WAY DOWN SOUTH
Southern Steam in the Sixties

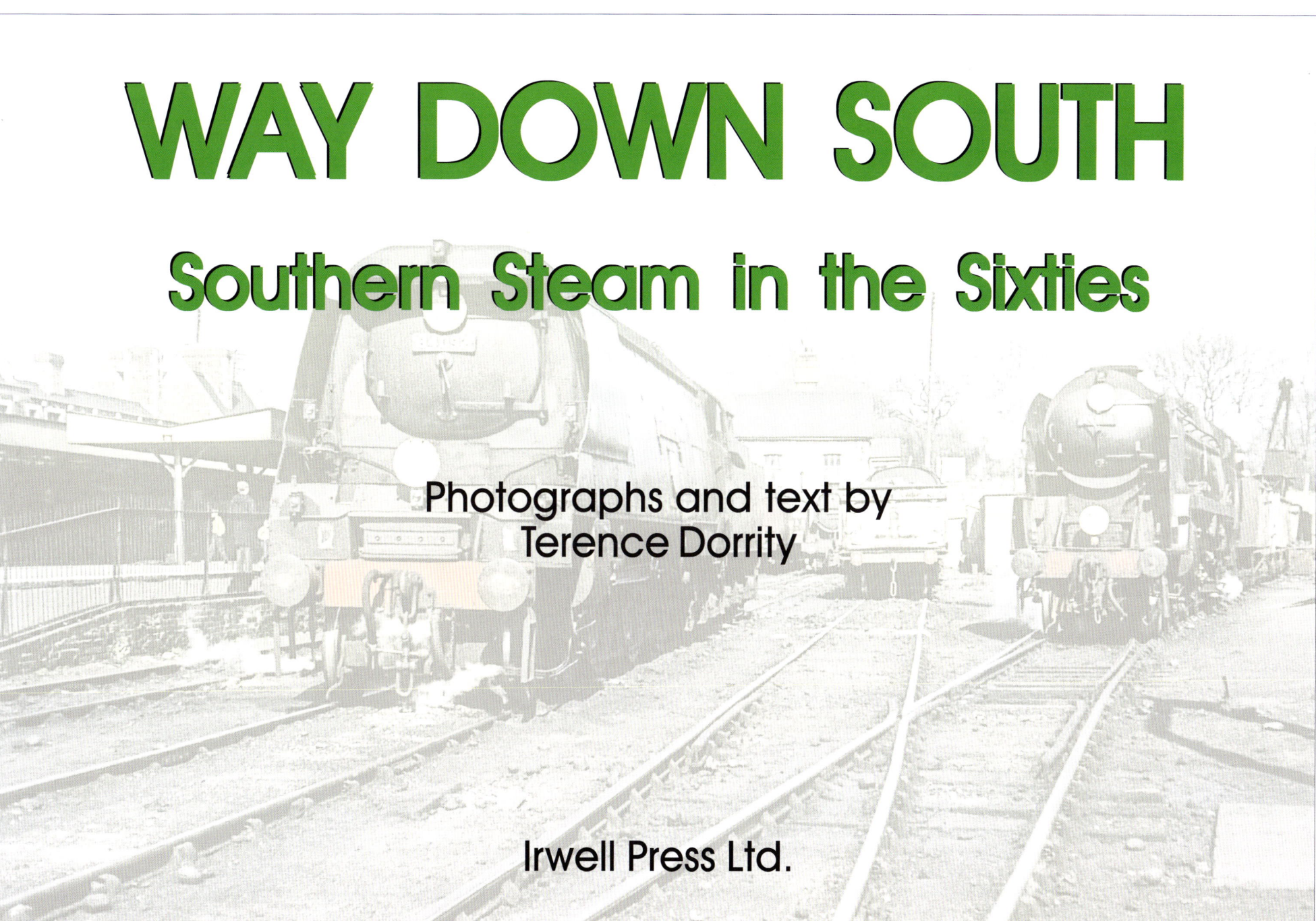

Photographs and text by
Terence Dorrity

Irwell Press Ltd.

WAY DOWN SOUTH

Southern Steam in the Sixties   Photographs by Terence Dorrity

For about a hundred and forty years thousands of steam locomotives hauled passenger and goods trains in almost every corner of Great Britain playing a pivotal role in the economic and social history of the country and in the 1960s, although nearing the end of their reign, they were still very much part of everyday life and the sight and sound of them was an integral feature of the rural and urban landscape. Like the steam, this sight has now evaporated and the photographs in this book are intended to evoke this scene: nostalgic to some, of historic interest to others.

In Britain in the 1950s and 1960s, groups of mainly young boys populated the ends of the platforms of many railway stations. I was one of them. The pursuit we were engaged in was at the time at least as popular as football, stamp collecting or any other hobby. It was so popular, indeed, that you were considered rather odd if you did not take part. And what was this strange pastime? Jotting down the numbers of railway engines! Until the beginning of the 1960s these were still mainly steam and thanks to the compact little books published by Ian Allan these "trainspotters" had comprehensive lists of the thousands of numbers of the over one hundred and fifty types, or classes, of steam locomotives in service. Apart from a few "standard" British Railways designs, these had all been inherited from the "Big Four" railway companies which had come together as British Railways on nationalisation on the first day of January 1948. Each of these railway companies had their own distinctive locomotive styles and also used many older locomotives which had belonged to the numerous constituent companies that had been amalgamated to create the "Big Four" in 1923. In the 1960s the British Railways Southern Region fleet consisted of examples from the London Brighton and South Coast Railway (LBSCR), the London and South Western Railway (LSWR) and the South Eastern and Chatham Railway (SECR) as well as types designed and built by the Southern Railway (SR) and a small number of dock shunters originally brought to England during the second World War by the United States Army Transportation Corps (USATC).

Until 1948 the "Big Four" companies had followed distinct practices, many of which still continued until well after nationalisation, but in 1955 the British Railways modernisation programme envisaged the replacement of steam by electric and diesel traction. The realisation that the railway scene was about to change forever prompted a number of erstwhile "trainspotters" who had become more serious railway enthusiasts to join the few old hands who were already doing so and record the historic last days of steam on film and, like them, in my teens and early twenties I followed up my initial interest and did the same.

I was able to amass a wide ranging collection of photographs documenting a once common sight which, with the exception of a number of preserved locomotives still in action, has now disappeared.

N class 2-6-0 31401 runs light past Reading South shed on Friday 1 January 1965.

I had been fascinated by steam locomotives from an early age. This probably had its origin when my mother took me to our local station at Henley-in-Arden to see the Royal Train go past. This was on the visit by King George VI, Queen Elizabeth and Princess Margaret to Stratford-upon-Avon on the 20 April 1950. I have since found out, thanks to the archive service of the Shakespeare Centre, that it was headed by two ex GWR "Castles", 5000 *Launceston Castle* and 5035 *Coity Castle*. The members of the Royal Family were not even on board at the time as the train was on its way to Tyseley for servicing but as I was just under four years old it was the royal engines that impressed me. A little later my paternal grandfather worked for Tothill Press in London. He was in the advertising department which presumably dealt with all their titles but one of them at that time was the "Railway Magazine" and he would give me a copy when I saw him. The points were set for an enduring interest.

Although I later lived in Stratford-upon-Avon my horizons were wider than the Western Region. I had a real fondness for the Southern Region because my grandparents and several uncles and aunts lived in or near Brighton and so I regularly visited the area. I remember being fascinated by the green electric trains and particularly impressed by the umber and cream "Brighton Belle" but a favourite spot was the view of the engine shed from Howard Place near the station and, among its treasures, the sight of a "Terrier" in Stroudley "improved engine green", in reality ochre, livery with "Brighton Works" painted on the tank sides. Unfortunately, by the time I was taking colour photographs and I caught up with it, 32635, at Eastleigh in April 1963 it had been withdrawn and its chimney had been removed. However, a number of ex LBSCR A1X tank engines were still at work for a little while longer. My long suffering father, not especially interested in steam, took me to see some of these just in time at the Lancing Carriage Works and at Havant where they were working the Hayling Island branch and these are well represented in this book.

There had been earlier holidays at Bournemouth with my mother but at that time I relied on a Kodak Brownie 127 camera and I still have some grainy black and white photographs taken then. It did mean I had the chance of going on a couple of day trips to the Isle of Wight and later I was determined to return with a better camera and some colour film. Fortunately little had changed when I was able to visit again in 1963 and 1964 and the results can be found in this book. I really do have to say "thanks Dad", and "thanks Mum" and this book is dedicated to both of them.

It was, perhaps, surprising that veteran steam engines were still to be found in a region which, with the notable exception of the ex LSWR main line from London Waterloo to Southampton and Bournemouth and the route west via Salisbury plus a few branch and secondary lines such as the one from Reading to Tonbridge, had been progressively electrified. Diesel locomotives and multiple units had also been constructed for the ex South Eastern Railway Hastings line and some other non-electrified routes. However, the use of third rail electrification meant that for reasons of safety some steam tank locomotives were retained in the early 1960s for use in goods yards and on trains linking them, in departmental service at a number of sites and on a few lightly used lines.

Probably the best known tank engine survivors were those employed in regular passenger service on branch lines associated by many with Summer holidays. These were the afore mentioned Hayling Island branch, with its ex LBSCR "Terriers", the Lymington and Swanage branches, usually operated by ex LSWR "M7" tanks, the Lyme Regis branch with the unusual LSWR "Radial" tanks, and the remaining lines on the Isle of Wight from Ryde to Cowes and Ventnor with the ex LSWR "O2"s. This last was something of a time capsule. Isolated from the rest of the system, and reachable on an ex Southern Railway paddle steamer, this fully steam operated system used a delightful collection of ex LBSCR and SECR carriages and nineteen locomotives. A number of the tank engines are still running today thanks to preservation movements in the region which were already active in the 1960s. The trailblazing Bluebell Railway ran its first train in 1960 and the Kent and East Sussex Railway, which did not start operating until the following decade, had started to collect suitable locomotives. Other lines have followed, notably the Swanage branch and a section of the Ryde to Cowes line on the Isle of Wight. Both have tank locomotives which ran on them in the 1960s in their collections.

For many, though, the main attraction of the Southern Region towards the end of steam was its fleet of powerful express passenger engines because during the early 1960s the top link 8P (the most powerful passenger) classified locomotives of the other three of the "Big Four" pre-nationalisation railways were being retired from service. The ex Great Western Region "King" and the ex London Midland and Scottish Railway "Princess" classes succumbed in 1962, a few ex LMSR "Coronation" Pacifics held out until 1964 and, with the exception of a handful of survivors in Scotland most famously A4s on Glasgow to Aberdeen expresses until mid 1966, numbers of the ex London and North Eastern Railway A1, A2 and A4 classes were dwindling fast. It was, however, still possible to witness "Merchant Navy" 8P Pacifics, along

That's the way to travel! Ex-Southern Railway PS Ryde on the Portsmouth to Ryde crossing.

with "West Country", "Battle of Britain" and some standard classes, doing exactly what Oliver Bulleid designed them for in regular action along the last predominately steam operated main line in the UK. This ran from Waterloo to Weymouth via Southampton and Bournemouth. Although diesel locomotives were increasingly employed, steam operation continued until Sunday 9 July 1967 when "Merchant Navy" 35030 *Elder Dempster Lines* brought the final regular steam hauled express into Waterloo in what is sometimes, rather obviously, referred to as the "Waterloo Sunset". The following day the "Bournemouth Electric" service was fully inaugurated and it was all over.

the countryside as they are unleashed to haul a train at speed on the main line. They are echoing, also, the last years of regular steam more than half a century ago.

With this book we can relive the sight of these workhorses undertaking their daily duties all those years ago and I hope it will evoke pleasant memories for those who remember them in action and that it will also be of interest to everyone who admires these magnificent machines. The Bulleid Pacifics are seen at several vantage points along the route from Waterloo to Weymouth and this is followed by a look at these classes elsewhere on the Southern Region network on the line via Salisbury and on special trains in other regions. Next, other Southern Railway tender locomotives that survived into the 1960s are depicted, particularly on the Reading to Redhill line which was steam operated until January 1965 using N and U class 2-6-0s. Of special interest is a venerable survivor, an ex SECR C class 0-6-0, which had become part of the departmental stock and was employed at Ashford Works. Tank classes are mainly shown at work on the branch lines mentioned before but also at other locations including sheds, works and early preservation sites. There are also some that had been sold for industrial use to private operators. The tank engines were almost all survivors from the pre-grouping railways and the photographs are arranged by company but ex USATC dock tanks built during the Second World War and two classes of BR standard tanks which were in common use in the region are also included. Finally, although ex LSWR locomotives, the O2 class examples at work on the Isle of Wight deservedly have a section of their own.

Left. Mamiya, Prismat CPH, 35mm SLR camera: Mamiya Sekor 1:1.9 48mm lens.
Centre. Kodak Retinette 35mm camera: Schneider-Kreuznach Reomar 1:3.5 45mm lens.
Right. Taron Marquise 35mm camera: Taronar 1:1.8 45mm lens.

It is not difficult to see members of the Bulleid Pacific locomotive classes today as twenty of the one hundred and ten "West Country" and "Battle of Britain" type and as many as eleven of the original thirty "Merchant Navy" class locomotives have survived into preservation, most of them having been recovered from the famous steam graveyard of Dai Woodham's scrapyard in Barry. Some are on public display, well cared for and polished but silent and lifeless and one even cut into sections, rather like the stuffed and mounted animals in a museum. Others are maintained in working order and pace up and down preserved lines where, although in action, they are confined like animals in a zoo. However, thanks to the hard work and dedication of enthusiasts, from time to time a few of these magnificent, powerful beasts can still be spotted in the wild and their roar can be heard echoing across

I had taken earlier black and white photographs with my trusty Kodak Brownie 127 roll film camera before I graduated to 35mm when I got a Kodak Retinette. Limited colour slide film followed in 1960 when the rather slow, but I now realise colour stable over time, 12 ASA Kodachrome was the most popular brand. This was replaced by Kodachrome II and Kodachrome X with, each time, an increase in ASA speed which was obviously useful when photographing moving trains. I tried other makes in small quantities, Ilford, Perutz, High Speed Ektachrome, but relied mainly on Kodakchrome and Agfa CT18. Earlier photos taken on Agfa film have lasted the fifty years or so reasonably well but some of the later ones have very annoyingly suffered badly from colour deterioration and can be grainy so have not been considered suitable for this book. I used the three different cameras shown in the picture over the period covered, the final one being the SLR.
Terence Dorrity 2018

CONTENTS

1: Pacific Power from Waterloo to Weymouth 6
Bulleid "Merchant Navy", "West Country" and "Battle of Britain" Pacifics all along the line

2: Wandering Pacifics 37
Bulleid Pacifics on the West Country main line to Salisbury and Yeovil and elsewhere

3: Other Southern Tender Engines 46
A miscellany of types in action and withdrawn.

4: Along the North Downs Line 58
U and N class 2-6-0 locomotives on Reading to Redhill services

5: Ex LBSCR Tank Engines 69
"Terriers" and other locomotives which passed from the LBSCR to the Southern Railway

6: Ex SECR, USA and BR Tank Engines 85
Including several SECR locomotives now preserved and some examples of BR standard tanks which were replacing Southern types

7: Ex LSWR Tank Engines 98
Including M7 0-4-4T locomotives on the Lymington and Swanage branches

8: Over the Water to the Isle of Wight 116
LSWR 02 class 0-4-4T locomotives and vintage carriages on the island

Merchant Navy Pacific 35023 HOLLAND-AFRIKA LINE passes Vauxhall station on Saturday 28 December 1963.

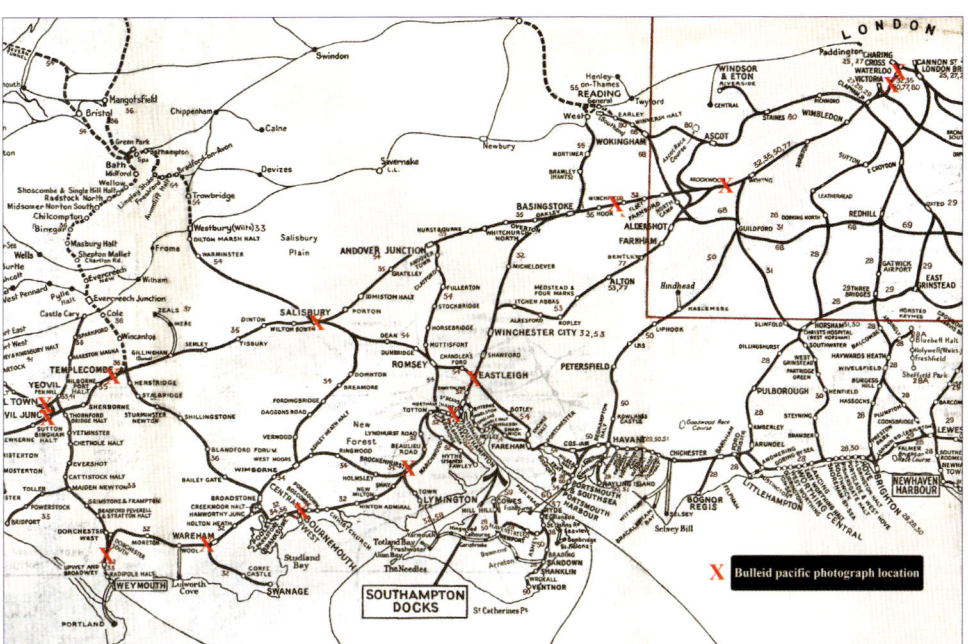

Route map from the Summer 1962 British Railways Southern Region timetable showing the locations of the Bulleid Pacific photographs taken along the ex London and South Western main line from Waterloo to Weymouth and the Exeter line as far as Yeovil. Lines west of Salisbury were transferred to the Western Region in 1963.

I kept detailed notes at the time I took the photographs and I found the following useful for additional information:

The relevant British Railways Southern Region timetables
Ian Allan abc of British Railways Locomotives: Part 2 Southern Region, Winter 1960/61
BR steam locomotive index: http://www.brdatabase.info
Rail UK: http://www.railuk.info
Six Bells Junction, the Railtour Files: www.sixbellsjunction.co.uk
The British Locomotive Shed Directory: Ninth Edition. F/LT Aidan L F Fuller ACA
and the websites of the preserved lines mentioned.

Copyright IRWELL PRESS LIMITED
ISBN-978-1-911262-18-3
First published in the United Kingdom in 2018
by Irwell Press Limited, 59A, High Street, Clophill,
Bedfordshire MK45 4BE
Printed by Ackcent Media, UK
Tel: 01525 861888
www.irwellpress.com

1: Pacific Power from Waterloo to Weymouth

Oliver Bulleid designed rebuilt West Country Pacific 34009 LYME REGIS pulls empty stock into Waterloo station on Sunday 7 June 1964. The massive 1936 built Waterloo concrete signal box, behind, was closed in 1990 when the Eurostar terminal was constructed. 34009 was built at Brighton Works with air-smoothed casing as 21C109 in 1945 and rebuilt with the casing removed in 1961. It was withdrawn in October 1966 and scrapped.

Merchant Navy Pacific 35018 BRITISH INDIA LINE and rebuilt West Country pacific 34031 TORRINGTON wait to depart from Waterloo station on Saturday 28 December 1963. 35018 was built at Eastleigh Works in 1945 as SR 21C18. It was rebuilt in 1956 and withdrawn in August 1964 but after around fifteen years in the Woodham Brothers scrap line at Barry it was bought for preservation. 34031 was built in 1946 at Brighton Works as SR 21C131 and rebuilt at Eastleigh Works in 1958. It was withdrawn in February 1965 and scrapped.

Rebuilt West Country Pacific 34031 TORRINGTON pulls away at Waterloo on Saturday 28 December 1963. 4 COR (Class 404) EMU 3150 waits at the next platform to leave on route 80, a Waterloo to Portsmouth Harbour semi-fast via Worplesdon stopping at Havant.

Unrebuilt West Country Pacific 34007 WADEBRIDGE approaches Vauxhall station on a Bournemouth West train on Saturday 28 December 1963. 34007 was built at Brighton Works as SR 21C107 and withdrawn in October 1965. It has been preserved and is normally to be found at the Mid-Hants "Watercress" Line. The eleven storey 1960s building on the left, Eastbury House on Albert Embankment, has been replaced by Merano Residences rising up to 28 storeys. The brick building to the right of the train has also been demolished.

35017 BELGIAN MARINE is welcomed to London by the then newish buildings along Albert Embankment and a distant "Whiteway's Devon Cyder" hoarding as it heads for Waterloo past Vauxhall station on Saturday 28 December 1963. One of a class of thirty designed by Oliver Bulleid, this Merchant Navy Pacific was built as 21C17 with air-smoothed casing at Eastleigh Works in 1945. It was rebuilt with the casing removed in in 1957 and withdrawn from service in July 1966 and scrapped.

Unrebuilt West Country Pacific 34015 EXMOUTH passes through Brookwood station on the down fast line at the head of a Fawley oil train on Saturday 25 July 1964. The wagons behind the locomotive are presumably barrier wagons to protect against fire. 34015 was built at Brighton Works as 21C115 in 1945 and was withdrawn in April 1967. Brookwood station, 28 miles from Waterloo, was opened by the London and South Western Railway in 1864 and rebuilt in 1903 when the track was quadrupled.

Named after the wartime Secretary of State for Air, rebuilt Battle of Britain Pacific 34059 SIR ARCHIBALD SINCLAIR passes Brookwood station on the down fast line on Saturday 25 July 1964. This train had left Waterloo at 17:00 and was due to arrive at Salisbury at 19:00. 34059 was built as 21C159 at Brighton Works in 1947. It was rebuilt in 1960 and withdrawn in May 1966. After a time in Woodham Brothers scrapyard at Barry it was bought for preservation and is now to be found on the Bluebell Railway.

Nine Elms (70A) allocated rebuilt West Country Pacific 34101 HARTLAND pulls into Brookwood Station on the Saturdays Only 17:54 stopping train from Waterloo to Basingstoke (arrive 19:14) on 25 July 1964. 34101 was one of only six of the class built at Eastleigh Works, in 1950, and it was rebuilt in 1960. It was withdrawn in July 1966 and, fortunately, after spending some time at Woodham Brothers scrapyard at Barry it is now preserved and based on the North Yorkshire Moors Railway.

Unrebuilt Battle of Britain Pacific 34064 FIGHTER COMMAND rushes by near Winchfield on Saturday 13 March 1965. This was the 08:35 departure from Waterloo with sections due to arrive at Bournemouth West at 11:33 and Weymouth at 12:34. Built at Brighton Works as 21C164, this locomotive was withdrawn in May 1966 and scrapped. These unrebuilt locomotives were sometimes unflatteringly called 'Spam Cans'.

Unrebuilt Battle of Britain Pacific 34063 229 SQUADRON runs along the up slow line in charge of a loaded ballast train just after the Totters Lane bridge between Hook and Winchfield on Saturday 13 March 1965. Could this have been carrying ballast from Meldon Quarry in Somerset? The discs indicate a train from the Salisbury line and further west.

Three and a half hours later 34063 229 SQUADRON passes by in the opposite direction near Winchfield on a longer, presumably empty, ballast train on Saturday 13 March 1965. 34063 was built as 21C163 at Brighton Works in 1947 and withdrawn in August 1965 and cut up.

Merchant Navy Pacific 35021 NEW ZEALAND LINE hurries by under the impressive Old Potbridge Road bridge between Hook and Winchfield on the up fast line on Saturday 13 March 1965. This was "The Royal Wessex" which had left Weymouth at 07:37 and had been joined at Bournemouth Central by the 08:20 from Bournemouth West. It was due to arrive at Waterloo at 10:50. 35021 was built at Eastleigh Works in 1948 and rebuilt in 1959. It was withdrawn in August 1965 and cut up.

Salisbury (70E) allocated unrebuilt West Country Pacific 34006 BUDE has just passed under the Old Potbridge Road bridge on the up slow line on Saturday 13 March 1965. The train had departed from Salisbury at 09:00 and was due to arrive at Waterloo at 11:26. The M3 motorway now crosses the line where this photograph was taken. BUDE was built at Brighton Works as 21C106 in 1945 and was withdrawn in March 1967 and scrapped.

Merchant Navy Pacific 35029 ELLERMAN LINES thunders by under the Old Potbridge Road bridge on the up fast line on Saturday 13 March 1965. This was the 09:21 Weymouth to Waterloo (arrive 12:46). The 10:08 Bournemouth West portion had been attached at Bournemouth Central. 35029 was built at Eastleigh Works in 1949 and was rebuilt in 1959. It was withdrawn in September 1966 and is now to be found as a sectioned exhibit at the National Railway Museum in York.

Merchant Navy Pacific 35007 ABERDEEN COMMONWEALTH hurries along on the down Bournemouth Belle Pullman train near Winchfield on Saturday 13 March 1965. It had left Waterloo at 12:30 and was due to arrive at Bournemouth West at 14:42. 35007 was built at Eastleigh Works as 21C7 in 1942 and it was rebuilt in 1958. It was withdrawn in July 1967 and scrapped. The Bournemouth Belle was introduced by the Southern Railway in 1931 and, except during wartime and until 1947, it ran right up to the end of locomotive hauled trains on the line on 9 July 1967.

Unrebuilt West Country Pacific 34038 LYNTON nears Winchfield on Saturday 13 March 1965. This was the 10:30 departure from Exeter St David's due to arrive at Waterloo at 14:13. LYNTON was built at Brighton Works as 21C138 in 1946 and was withdrawn in June 1966 and cut up.

Rebuilt West Country Pacific 34095 BRENTOR passes by near Winchfield on Saturday 13 March 1965. This train had departed from Weymouth at 11:30 with another section leaving Bournemouth West at 12:20. It was due to arrive at Waterloo at 14:40. 34095 was built at Eastleigh Works in 1949, rebuilt in 1961 and withdrawn in July 1967. It was cut up at Cashmore's at Newport the following April.

Rebuilt Battle of Britain class 34052 LORD DOWDING rushes past near Winchfield on Saturday 13 March 1965 on the Saturdays Only 13:24 stopping train from Waterloo which was due to arrive at Salisbury at 16:00. The leading Bulleid three coach set is 814. 34052 was built as 21C52 at Brighton Works in 1946 and rebuilt at Eastleigh Works in 1958. It was withdrawn in July 1967 and scrapped the following February at Cashmore's at Newport.

Rebuilt West Country Pacific 34024 TAMAR VALLEY is seen from the Old Potbridge Road bridge on Thursday 6 July 1967. This was the 08:46 from Bournemouth Central, Bournemouth West had closed in September 1965, which was due to arrive at Waterloo at 11:54. 34024 had hauled the last down steam Bournemouth Belle the day before. This was really the last gasp as steam ended on the Southern Region three days later, on 9 July 1967. 34024 was built at Brighton in 1946 as 21C124 and rebuilt in 1961. It was withdrawn in July 1967 and cut up at Cashmore's at Newport the following March. The third rail had been installed ready for the electric service but although the end was near locomotives were still attaining speeds in the high nineties and, it is claimed, occasionally just over one hundred miles an hour.

Unrebuilt Battle of Britain Pacific 34078 222 SQUADRON hurries through Eastleigh station on the down fast line on Tuesday 23 April 1963. The headcode suggests it was a special boat train from Waterloo to Southampton Docks. 34078 was built at Brighton Works in 1948 and withdrawn in September 1964 and scrapped. The station was opened by the LSWR in 1839 as Bishopstoke. It was later renamed Bishopstoke Junction, then Eastleigh and Bishopstoke before becoming Eastleigh in 1923.

Unrebuilt West Country Pacific 34038 LYNTON looks very smart and possibly ex works on its home shed, Eastleigh (71A), on Monday 28 August 1961. Built at Brighton Works in 1946 as 21C138, it was withdrawn in June 1966 and cut up at Cashmore's of Newport a few months later.

Rebuilt West Country Pacific 34098 TEMPLECOMBE stands in steam on Eastleigh shed (71A), where it was allocated, on Tuesday 23 April 1963. It was built at Brighton Works in 1949, rebuilt in 1961 and withdrawn to be scrapped in June 1967. The 15-road engine shed, opened in 1903, was closed in 1967.

The plates of 35013 BLUE FUNNEL CERTUM PETE FINEM await re-attachment to the locomotive at Eastleigh Works on Sunday 15 March 1964. The locomotive was built at Eastleigh Works as 21C13 in 1945, rebuilt in 1956 and was withdrawn in July 1967. The Latin phrase translates as Aim for a definite destination which is certainly a reassuring motto for a shipping line.

Time to get back on board the Home Counties Railway Society S&D special hauled by 35005 CANADIAN PACIFIC during a five minute stop at Southampton Central on Sunday 7 June 1964. The train ran from London Waterloo to Bournemouth Central and then along the S&D to Blandford Forum, Evercreech Junction, Highbridge and Bath Green Park. It then continued to Gloucester Eastgate and London Paddington using a range of motive power including two castles and S&D 2-8-0 53807. 35005 was built at Eastleigh Works in 1949 as 21C5. It was rebuilt and its streamlining removed in 1959 and was withdrawn in October 1965. It is now preserved and based on the Mid Hants Railway.

Exmouth Junction (72A) allocated unrebuilt West Country Pacific 34020 SEATON oozes steam as it rushes through Brockenhurst on the way to Bournemouth on Sunday 15 March 1964. The photograph was taken from the signal box at the A337 Lymington Road level crossing. 34020 was built at Brighton Works as 21C120 in 1945 and withdrawn in September 1964. The goods shed to the right is now the Porterhouse steak and fish restaurant.

Rebuilt West Country Pacific 34008 PADSTOW, rebuilt Battle of Britain Pacific 34050 ROYAL OBSERVER CORPS and standard class 4 4-6-0 75068 await their turn on Bournemouth shed (71B) on Sunday 7 June 1964. This photo was taken from the Home Counties Railway Society Somerset & Dorset tour train while it stopped at Bournemouth Central station. 34008 was built at Brighton Works in 1945 as 21C108 and was withdrawn in June 1967. 34050 was also built at Brighton Works, in 1946 as 21C150, and was withdrawn in August 1965. The shed closed in June 1967 and the site is now the station car park.

A very grimy Merchant Navy Pacific, 35027 PORT LINE, heads the 05:40 Waterloo to Weymouth, where it was due to arrive at 10:07, through Worgret Junction on Wednesday 8 April 1964. It was running about 10 minutes late. The line nearest the camera is the Swanage branch. 35027 was built at Eastleigh Works in 1948 and was rebuilt in 1959. It was withdrawn in August 1965 and is now preserved. Behind the tender is a typical Southern CCT parcels van.

Rebuilt Battle of Britain Pacific 34088 213 SQUADRON has just passed Worgret Junction signal box on the 08:35 Waterloo to Weymouth, where it was due to arrive at 12:34, on Wednesday 8 April 1964. 34088 was built at Brighton Works in 1948, rebuilt in 1960 and was withdrawn from service in March 1967 and scrapped.

Merchant Navy Pacific 35029 ELLERMAN LINES approaches Worgret Junction on the 11:30 Weymouth to Waterloo (arrive 14:40) on Wednesday 8 April 1964. This train would link up with a Bournemouth West section at Bournemouth Central. 35029 was built at Eastleigh Works in 1949 and was rebuilt in 1959. It was withdrawn in September 1966 and is now a sectioned exhibit at the National Railway Museum in York.

Merchant Navy Pacific 35021 NEW ZEALAND LINE passes over Worgret Junction on the 12:10 stopping train from Weymouth to Bournemouth (arrive 13:33) on Wednesday 8 April 1964. 35021 was built at Eastleigh Works in 1948 and rebuilt in 1959. It was withdrawn in August 1965 and cut up.

Unrebuilt Battle of Britain class 34066 SPITFIRE heads a Weymouth to Bristol train in the Ridgeway Cutting just before entering Bincombe Tunnel on Sunday 5 September 1965. The train was being banked up the 1 in 50 incline by standard class 4 2-6-0 76014. This was the 16:35 from Weymouth which ran via Yeovil and Westbury and was due to arrive at Bristol Temple Meads at 19:16. 34066 was built at Brighton Works as 21C166 in 1947 and was withdrawn in September 1966 and scrapped.

2: Wandering Pacifics

Unrebuilt West Country Pacific 34030 WATERSMEET starts off at Templecombe on Wednesday 8 April 1964. This was the stopping section of the 15:00 from Waterloo to Exeter Central which was due to arrive there at 19:31. The train had split at Templecombe and the fast train, which arrived at Exeter at 18:31, had already departed. 34030 was built at Brighton Works in 1946 as SR 21C130 and was withdrawn in September 1964. The station, originally opened by the Salisbury and Yeovil Railway in 1860, was closed in 1966 and reopened in 1983.

Unrebuilt West Country Pacific 34092 CITY OF WELLS and rebuilt West Country Pacific 34010 SIDMOUTH stand on Yeovil Town shed on Wednesday 8 April 1964. 34092 was built at Brighton Works in 1949 and withdrawn in November 1964. It is now preserved. 34010 was also a Brighton product, built in 1945 as SR 21C110. It was withdrawn in March 1965 and, like 34092, is now preserved. The shed had been Southern Region 72C but was recoded 83E when transferred to the Western Region in September 1963. It was closed in June 1965 and, along with the adjacent station, is now the site of a cinema and leisure centre.

Rebuilt Battle of Britain Pacific 34052 LORD DOWDING, named after the Air Officer Commanding RAF Fighter Command during the Battle of Britain, pulls into Yeovil Junction station while ex GWR 0-6-0PT 6435 waits to leave on the 15:50 auto train for Yeovil Town on Wednesday 8 April 1964. 34052 was at the head of the 13:00 Waterloo departure which continued to Exeter Central and Plymouth where it was due to arrive at 18:54. It was built at Brighton Works in 1946 as SR 21C152, rebuilt in 1958 and withdrawn in July 1967 and cut up.

Merchant Navy Pacific 35025 BROCKLEBANK LINE takes on water in front of the coaling stage at Salisbury shed (72B) on Sunday 4 June 1961. It was built at Eastleigh in 1945, rebuilt with the casing removed in 1956 and withdrawn in September 1964. It is now preserved.

Battle of Britain Pacific 34089 602 SQUADRON on Brighton shed (75A) on Sunday 21 April 1963. Built at Brighton Works in 1948 and rebuilt in 1960, it was withdrawn July 1967 and scrapped. In the early 1950s it had been one of a small number of these locomotives allocated for a few months to the Eastern Region Stratford shed (30A).

34045 OTTERY ST MARY climbing Hatton Bank on a football special is about to pass a 9F 2-10-0 in charge of a southbound freight on Saturday 27 April 1963. This was one of many specials from Southampton for the FA cup semi-final between Manchester United and Southampton played at Villa Park which brought about a dozen Bulleid Pacifics to Birmingham. It was scheduled to leave Southampton at 09:10 and arrive at Birmingham Snow Hill at 13:11, though it was eleven minutes late! Man United, with a team including Bobby Charlton and Nobby Stiles, won 1-0 with the goal scored by Denis Law.

34094 MORTEHOE stands next to A4 class 60029 WOODCOCK on Doncaster shed (36A) on Sunday 12 May 1963. It had arrived on a Warwickshire Railway Society special which ran from Birmingham New Street to visit Derby Works and shed (17A), Doncaster Works and shed and Barrow Hill shed (41E). 34094 was built at Brighton Works in 1949 and was withdrawn in August 1964. 60029 was built at Doncaster Works in 1937 as LNER 4493. It was withdrawn in October 1963.

Unrebuilt Battle of Britain class 34051 WINSTON CHURCHILL passes by on Churchill's funeral train near Radley on Saturday 30 January 1965. It was on its way from Waterloo to Hanborough, the nearest station to Bladon parish church where Churchill was to be buried. The steam is hiding the first carriage, Pullman brake car 208, and most of the now preserved hearse van S2464S. Pullman kitchen-parlour cars CARINA and LYDIA, seen in the photograph, were followed by Pullman parlour car PERSEUS and Pullman brake car ISLE OF THANET. Note the locomotive headcode discs which formed a "V"- for Victory.

34051 WINSTON CHURCHILL was in charge of the Stephenson Locomotive Society (Midland Area) "The Bulleid Pacific Rail Tour" at Harbury in better weather on Sunday 23 May 1965. The tour had started at Birmingham Snow Hill and ran to Oxford, Salisbury, Exeter Central, Westbury, Bath Spa, Gloucester Eastgate, Kidderminster and back to Snow Hill. Other locomotives used on the tour were 35017 BELGIAN MARINE and 7029 CLUN CASTLE. 34051 was built at Brighton Works in 1946 as 21C151 and was withdrawn in September 1965 just eight months after it had hauled Sir Winston Churchill's funeral train. Fortunately, it is now preserved and is part of the national collection.

3: Other Southern Tender Engines

N15 "King Arthur" class 4-6-0 30800 SIR MELEAUS DE LILE sidelined at Eastleigh shed (71A) on Monday 28 August 1961. Although a Robert Urie London and South Western Railway design, this locomotive entered service with Richard Maunsell modifications after the grouping as Southern Railway 800. It was built at Eastleigh Works in 1926 and withdrawn in the month this photograph was taken. It was scrapped during the following month.

Basingstoke (70D) allocated N15 "King Arthur" class 4-6-0 30793 SIR ONTZLAKE at Nine Elms (70A) on Sunday 15 July 1962. Behind it is one of the five ex Great Western Railway 5700 class 0-6-0PT locomotives allocated there at the time for stock working into Waterloo and there is an E4 on the next road. 30793 was built at Eastleigh Works in 1926 and withdrawn the month after this photograph was taken.

N15 "King Arthur" class 4-6-0 30768 SIR BALIN is in steam at Eastleigh shed (71A) on Monday 28 August 1961. This locomotive entered service in 1925 as SR 768. It was one of thirty of the class built by the North British Locomotive Company of Glasgow which were sometimes nicknamed "Scotch Arthurs". Another forty-four were built at Eastleigh Works. 30768 was withdrawn, from Eastleigh shed, just two months after this photograph was taken. Note the eight wheel bogie tender.

S15 4-6-0 30823 passing through Brookwood station in the early evening of Saturday 25 July 1964; the headcode suggests a Nine Elms-Plymouth working. This was the first of the post-grouping Maunsell modified Southern Railway examples of the LSWR Robert Urie designed class, built at Eastleigh Works in 1927. It was withdrawn in November 1964. Note the station sign on the right, NECROPOLIS BROOKWOOD CEMETERY. At one time there was a branch line into the cemetery with two stations, Cemetery North for Non-Conformists and Cemetery South for Anglicans, with dedicated funeral trains running from London Necropolis station, near Waterloo.

30692 simmers on Salisbury shed (72B) on Sunday 4 June 1961. This Dugald Drummond designed LSWR 700 class 0-6-0 was one of a class of thirty built primarily for goods train working by Dübs & Co as LSWR 692 in 1897. It was withdrawn in February 1962 and scrapped during the following month.

Oliver Bulleid designed wartime "Austerity" Q1 class 0-6-0 33003 and ex GWR 0-6-0PT 4681 stand alongside Feltham shed (70B) on Sunday 7 July 1963. Built at Brighton in 1942 as C3, 33003 was withdrawn in June 1964. Twenty of this class of forty were built at Brighton Works and the rest at Ashford Works. The six road Feltham shed closed in 1967.

Q1 class 33035 runs round at Bordon on the Railway Enthusiasts' Club "Hampshire Hog" railtour on a very rainy Saturday 14 March 1964. The tour ran via Aldershot, Bordon, Alton, Winchester City, Eastleigh, Winchester Chesil, Newbury, Didcot, Reading General, Ascot, Chertsey and Woking to Farnborough Main first behind the Q1 to Eastleigh and then 41329, an Ivatt 2MT 2-6-2 tank locomotive. Bordon station was opened by the LSWR in 1905 but it was closed to passengers in 1957. It finally closed to goods traffic two years after this photograph was taken. 33035 was built at Ashford Works as C35 in 1942 and withdrawn in October 1964.

Late snow still lies on the ground as U 2-6-0 31639 leads Q1 0-6-0 33006 along the Stratford and Midland Junction line, about to pass under the B4451 Kineton to Southam road bridge, on Sunday 7 March 1965. The train is the Home Counties Railway Society "Six Counties Railtour".

The view now is from the A41 Warwick to Banbury road bridge with 31639 and 33006 approaching Burton Dassett signal box on the "Six Counties Railtour". This was where the former Edge Hill Light Railway branched off, to the left. The tour ran from Paddington to Fenny Compton, then along the SMJ to Stratford-upon-Avon and on to Wellingborough via Leamington Spa, Rugby and Northampton. It returned to Paddington via Bedford, Bletchley, Bicester and Oxford.

Wainwright C class 0-6-0 DS239 busily shunting at Ashford Works on Tuesday 20 September 1966. Built at Longhedge Works as SECR 592 in 1902, it was withdrawn from regular service as BR 31592 in July 1963 and became departmental DS 239 for use at Ashford Works.

Another view of the venerable DS239 at Ashford Works on Tuesday 20 September 1966. It was the last survivor of a class of 109 locomotives built at the SECR Longhedge and Ashford Works and also by Neilson, Reid & Co and Sharp Stewart & Co. It was bought for preservation by members of the the Wainwright 'C' Preservation Society at the end of 1969 and is now to be found looking much smarter on the Bluebell Railway.

Billinton ex London Brighton and South Coast Railway K class 2-6-0 32338 awaits its end at the head of a line of withdrawn locomotives at Hove goods yard on Tuesday 16 April 1963. "Schools" class 30923 BRADFIELD is behind. 32338 was built at Brighton Works as 338 in 1913 and withdrawn in December 1962.

Richard Maunsell designed U1 class 31895 also waits for the cutters torch at Hove goods yard on Tuesday 16 April 1963. It was built at Eastleigh Works in 1931 and withdrawn in December 1962. Twenty-one examples of this three-cylinder development of the two-cylinder U class were built. The Dubarry Perfumery Company Ltd building behind with its ornate Art Deco style mosaic panels has now become the Hove Business Centre.

Richard Maunsell designed three-cylinder V class "Schools" 4-4-0 30901 WINCHESTER in the long line of other locomotives at Hove goods yard on Tuesday 16 April 1963 is clearly never going to steam again. 30901 was built at Eastleigh Works in 1930 and was withdrawn in December 1962.

N class 2-6-0 31401 waits for duty in steam on Brighton shed (75A) on Sunday 21 April 1963. It was one of 80 of this class originally designed for the SECR by Richard Maunsell but 31401 was built as Southern Railway 1401 in 1932 as part of a batch of fifteen constructed at Ashford Works after the grouping. It was withdrawn in July 1965 and scrapped by Cashmore's of Newport.

4: Along the North Downs Line

Six months before it was withdrawn, and looking dirtier than at Brighton two years earlier, N class 2-6-0 31401 had been re-allocated to the Reading to Redhill services. It is seen here running light past Reading South shed on New Year's Day 1965. This was just three days before diesel units were introduced on the line and the shed closed to steam.

N class 31401 near Wokingham on the 12:47 from Reading General which was due to arrive at Guildford at 13:42 on Friday 1 January 1965. Southern Region trains had been diverted from Reading Southern into the ex GWR Reading General station the previous September.

N class 31870 pulls away from Ash station in the rain on the 09:10 Reading Southern to Redhill, where it was due to arrive at 10:06, on Saturday 14 March 1964. It was built at Ashford Works as SR 1870 and entered service in 1925. It was withdrawn in April 1964 and cut up.

N class 31410 pulls into Crowthorne station on Tuesday 18 August 1964 in charge of the 13:35 Redhill to Reading Southern (arrive 15:18). The station was opened by the South Eastern Railway in 1859 as "Wellington College for Crowthorne", the college having contributed to the cost of construction. It was renamed "Crowthorne" in 1928. 31410 was built at Ashford Works as SR 1410 and entered service in 1933. It was withdrawn in November 1964 and scrapped.

U class 31800 arrives at North Camp station on a local passenger train on Sunday 26 July 1964. This was the 11:50 departure from Reading Southern which was due to arrive at Redhill at 13:44. 31800 was originally built at Brighton Works in 1926 as SECR K class 2-6-4T A800 RIVER CRAY and it was rebuilt as U class 2-6-0 1800 at Ashford Works in 1928. It was withdrawn in October 1965. The leading coach set, 456, consisted of Maunsell corridor brake second S3711S coupled to corridor composite S5629S.

Another view of 31800 at North Camp station on the 11:50 departure from Reading Southern on Sunday 26 July 1964. The lattice upper quadrant signal is off and there is a typical swan-neck gas lamp with a barley twist post on the other platform. As K class 2-6-4T A800 RIVER CRAY, this locomotive was involved in a serious accident at Sevenoaks in 1927 blamed on poor track and the unstable running of the locomotive. As a result the decision was taken to rebuild the class as 2-6-0 tender engines.

U class 2-6-0 31790 waits to depart from North Camp station on the 14:05 departure from Redhill which was due to arrive at Reading Southern at 15:45 on Sunday 26 July 1964. 31790 was originally built by the SECR as the first K class 2-6-4T 790 RIVER AVON in 1917 but it was rebuilt as a U class 2-6-0 at Eastleigh Works in 1928. It was withdrawn in May 1965. The station opened in 1858 as North Camp, Aldershot.

U class 31627 hurries by near Wokingham on the 12:05 departure from Reading General which was due to arrive at Redhill at 13:46 on Friday 1 January 1965. It was built at Ashford Works in 1929 and withdrawn in October 1965.

U class 31791 on a short goods train heads towards Guildford through Crowthorne station on Tuesday 18 August 1964. It entered service in 1925 as K class 2-6-4T A791 RIVER ADUR built by Armstrong Whitworth but it was rebuilt three years later as U class 2-6-0 1791 at Eastleigh Works.

Five months later U class 31791 passes by near Wokingham in charge of a single guards van in the early afternoon on Friday 1 January 1965. It was not to be a Happy New Year for steam on the line as it was very soon to come to an end. 31791 was one of the last two of the class to be withdrawn, from Guildford shed (70C), in June 1966 and it was cut up at Cashmore's of Newport shortly afterwards.

With only three days to go before class 206 diesel-electric multiple units take over the service, and in light appropriate to the "sunset of steam", U class 31809 scurries past near Wokingham on the 13:35 departure from Redhill which was due to arrive at Reading General at 15:18 on Friday 1 January 1965. It was built at Brighton Works as K class A809 RIVER DART in 1926 and it was rebuilt as a U class at Brighton Works as SR Number 1809 in 1928 and withdrawn in January 1966.

5: Ex LBSCR Tank Engines

London Brighton and South Coast Railway William Stroudley designed A1X class 0-6-0T DS681 stands out of steam at the ex LBSCR Lancing Carriage Works on Thursday 18 April 1963. It was originally built as an A1 class at Brighton in 1875 as 59 CHEAM but it was rebuilt as an A1X in 1921. It had become BR number 32659 before being renumbered to service stock as DS681 in 1953. It was scrapped at Eastleigh in June 1963 and so, unlike most of the class which survived into the 1960s, it was not preserved. Opened in January 1912, the carriage works closed on 25 June 1965.

A1X 32662 is busily at work at Lancing Carriage Works on Thursday 18 April 1963. Built at Brighton as A1 class 62 MARTELLO in 1875, it was rebuilt in 1912. When it was withdrawn, in November 1963, it was sold to Butlin's for display at the Ayr holiday camp along with ex LMSR pacific 6233 DUCHESS OF SUTHERLAND. In 1971 it went to the Bressingham Steam Museum where it has been displayed as 662 MARTELLO and as 32662.

A1X 32636 at Lancing Carriage Works on Thursday 18 April 1963. Built as A1 class 72 FENCHURCH at Brighton in 1872, it was sold to the Newhaven Harbour Company in June 1898 and acquired by the Southern Railway in 1926. It was withdrawn by BR in January 1964 and sold for preservation to the Bluebell Railway. Locomotives of this class were often called "Terriers" or "Rooters".

A1X 32640 at Brighton (75A) shed on Sunday 21 April 1963. It was built as A1 class 40 BRIGHTON in 1878 and it was sent to represent the LBSCR at the 1878 Paris exhibition where it was awarded a gold medal for its design. It was sold to the Isle of Wight Central Railway in 1901 and renumbered 11. In 1918 it was rebuilt as an A1X and at the grouping in 1923 became W11 on the Southern Railway and was later named NEWPORT. It was transferred back to the mainland in 1947 and, as BR 32640, was withdrawn in September 1963 and sold to Butlin's for display next to ex LMSR pacific 6203 PRINCESS MARGARET ROSE at the Pwllheli holiday camp. In 1973 it went to the Isle of Wight Steam Railway where it is now to be seen as W11 NEWPORT once again.

A1X 32646 stands in front of Newhaven shed on Tuesday 16 April 1963. It was built as an A1 at Brighton Works in 1877 with the number 46 and named NEWINGTON. It was rebuilt as an A1X in 1932. It had been sold to the Freshwater, Yarmouth and Newport Railway in March 1914 as 734 and it had become 2 when absorbed into the Southern Railway at the grouping in 1923. It was given the name FRESHWATER with the number W2 and later W8 before returning to the mainland as BR 32646 in 1949. Note the spark arrestor over the chimney. Newhaven was a sub-shed of Brighton (75A) and it was closed at the end of September 1963.

32646 looks very different at Hayling Island four and a half years later, on Friday 6 October 1967. It had been withdrawn from BR service in November 1963 and sold to Brickwoods Brewery in Portsmouth for display on a plinth outside the Hayling Billy public house painted in Stroudley livery and named NEWINGTON again. In 1979 it was donated to the Isle of Wight Locomotive Society at Havenstreet and restored to working order as W8 FRESHWATER.

A1X 32678 takes on water at Havant station in preparation to head its train along the 4½ mile branch to Hayling Island on Monday 22 April 1963. It was built at Brighton in 1880 as 78 KNOWLE and rebuilt as an A1X in 1911. It later went to the Isle of Wight and became W4 and later W14 BEMBRIDGE.

32678 heads the branch train across the level crossing at Langston (without a final "e") Halt on Monday 22 April 1963. When it was withdrawn, just six months after this photograph was taken, it was sold to Butlin's and put on display at the Minehead holiday camp alongside ex LMSR pacific 6229 DUCHESS OF HAMILTON. It was resold to the West Somerset Railway in 1975 but it is now to be found as 8 KNOWLE on the Kent & East Sussex Railway, at times carrying the number 32678 again.

32678 runs round past the coaling stage at Hayling Island station to take the train back on its thirteen minute run to Havant on Monday 22 April 1963. Locomotives of this class were retained for use on this line until it closed on 4 November 1963 because of weight restrictions on the timber Langstone (with a final "e" unlike the official name of the halt!) Harbour viaduct.

A1X 32670 at Eastleigh shed (71A) on Sunday 15 March 1964. It had been withdrawn the previous November. It was built as an A1 in 1872 as 70 POPLAR and sold to the Rother Valley Railway in 1901 where it became 3 BODIAM. Although it was rebuilt as an A1X in 1943, it did not become a Southern Railway locomotive but part of the BR Southern Region fleet on nationalisation in 1948.

32670 under restoration at the Kent and East Sussex Railway depot at Rolvenden on Tuesday 20 September 1966. After it was taken out of BR service, in 1963, it was sold to the Kent & East Sussex Preservation Society in April 1964 and it has become 3 BODIAM on that line once again.

A1X 55 STEPNEY at Sheffield Park on the Bluebell Railway with a Jaguar mark 1 and a Ford Prefect parked nearby on Sunday 21 April 1963. It was built at Brighton Works in 1875 and when it was withdrawn by BR in 1960, as 32655, it was bought by the Bluebell Railway and given its original identity as 55 STEPNEY and repainted in the LBSCR Stroudley "Improved Engine Green" livery, which, as can be seen, is not really green at all. It is said that Stroudley was colour blind.

Ex LBSCR E1 class 0-6-0T B110 at the Railway Preservation Society Hednesford site on Saturday 11 January 1964. It was built at Brighton Works in 1877 as 110 BURGUNDY. The last E1 in BR service was withdrawn in 1961 but fortunately BURGUNDY had been sold to the Cannock and Rugeley Colliery Company in 1927 where it became 9 CANNOCK WOOD. When no longer required, it was saved by the RPS in 1964. It later went to the East Somerset Railway and it is now to be found on the Isle of Wight Steam Railway where it has yet another identity as W2 YARMOUTH after one of four of the class that worked on the island, withdrawn in 1956.

Robert Billinton designed LBSCR E6 class 0-6-2 tank locomotive 32417 is in the company of other withdrawn locomotives at Hove goods yard on Tuesday 16 April 1963. Built in 1905 at Brighton Works as one of a class of ten, it had been withdrawn at the same time as two other last of the class the previous December.

Robert Billinton designed LBSCR Brighton built E4 class 0-6-2 radial tank locomotive 32468 at Hove goods yard among a number of withdrawn locomotives on Tuesday 16 April 1963. It entered service as 468 MIDHURST in 1898 and had been withdrawn, from Brighton shed, in January 1963 after it had gone through the buffers at Kemp Town and damaged the station building while it was working the 8 am goods from Brighton. It was replaced on local duties by sister E4 32479 which was reinstated in service having already been withdrawn.

E4 class 32479 in steam at Newhaven shed on Tuesday 16 April 1963. Built at Brighton Works in 1898 as 479 BEVENDEAN, it had been withdrawn in December 1962 and placed in the Hove goods yard scrap line but because of the accident with sister locomotive 32468 it re-entered service for a further six months working around Newhaven and Lewis and on the locally named "Lancing Belle" which conveyed workmen from Brighton to Lancing carriage works. It was finally withdrawn, the last of this class of seventy-five, from Brighton shed about seven weeks after this photograph was taken.

E4 class 473 BIRCH GROVE waits to depart from Horsted Keynes on the Bluebell Railway on Sunday 21 April 1963. This was soon after Bluebell trains were allowed into the station and just six months before the end of British Railways services from there to Haywards Heath via Ardingly. Built at Brighton Works in 1898, the locomotive became BR 32473. It was withdrawn in October 1962 but was bought for preservation. The carriage is Metropolitan Railway "Chesham" brake third No 307 with ventilators which were added in 1907-8 and which have since been removed when the Chesham set was fully restored.

6: Ex SECR, USA and BR Tank Engines

Harry Wainwright designed South Eastern and Chatham Railway P class 0-6-0 tank locomotive 27 glints in the late afternoon sunshine at Sheffield Park on Sunday 27 October 1968. Built as one of a small class of eight at Ashford Works in 1910, it was withdrawn from BR service as 31027 in 1961 and was bought for preservation on the Bluebell Railway where it at first became 27 PRIMROSE. By the time this photograph was taken it had been repainted in SECR livery and the name removed.

Ex SECR P class PIONEER II was one of two standard gauge locomotives at Bowaters Pulp and Paper Mills Ridham Dock on Monday 30 December 1963. It was built as 178 at Ashford Works in 1910 and it became Southern Railway 1178 at the grouping in 1923 and, later, BR 31178. It was, at times, hired to Bowater's and when withdrawn by BR, in 1958, it was sold to the company for use on the internal standard gauge branch to Ridham Dock where it worked until 1969 when it was acquired by the Bluebell Railway where it is based today. The 0-4-0ST behind, JUBILEE, was built in 1936 by W G Bagnall of Stafford (works number 2542) and is now preserved at the East Anglian Railway Museum at Chappel and Wakes Colne.

P class 323 BLUEBELL pulls into Sheffield Park on the Bluebell Railway on Saturday 28 April 1962. Built at Ashford Works in 1910 and withdrawn as BR 31323 in July 1960, it was bought for preservation on the Bluebell Railway where it became 323 and was named BLUEBELL for a number of years. Trains at the time were "top and tailed" with a locomotive at each end as they were not allowed into Horsted Keynes until later in the year and there were no run round facilities at the temporary terminus at Bluebell Halt. The carriages were the Metropolitan Railway "Chesham" set.

P class PRIDE OF SUSSEX at James Hodson & Sons flour mill at Robertsbridge on Tuesday 20 September 1966. It was built at Ashford Works in 1908 with the number 753 but it was requisitioned during the First World War by the Railway Operating Division (ROD) in 1915. It later became Southern Railway 556 and BR 31556 and was sold to Hodson's when it was withdrawn from BR service in April 1961. When no longer required, in 1970, it was bought by the Kent and East Sussex Railway, where it had previously worked on hire from the Southern Railway for three short periods before and after the war, and it became number 11. Next to it is a Humber Super Snipe with its innovative twin headlights.

On a glorious day, Tuesday 20 September 1966, Harry Wainwright designed ex SECR H class 0-4-4T 31263 was at the Kent and East Sussex Railway at Robertsbridge. One of a class of 66, it was built at Ashford Works as 263 in 1905. Three members of the class had remained at Three Bridges shed (75E) after the rest were withdrawn to work local trains to Tunbridge Wells until it was their turn in January 1964. One of these, 31263, was bought for preservation by the H-Class Trust and is now based on the Bluebell Railway.

USA class 30070, like 30065 next to it, had clearly been withdrawn from service at Eastleigh on Tuesday 23 April 1963 before transfer to departmental stock and allocation to Ashford Works. Both were built at Vulcan Ironworks (USA) in 1943. Fifteen of this United States Army Transportation Corps S100 0-6-0T type were purchased by the Southern Railway after the end of World War Two. 30070 had been WD1960 and 30065 WD1968.

Three and a half years later, on Tuesday 20 September 1966, USA class 30070, with its new identity DS238 WAINWRIGHT, looks in much better condition at work at Ashford Works. It had been renumbered and transferred to departmental stock in 1963. It was painted green and named WAINWRIGHT after the first locomotive superintendent of the SECR.

WAINWRIGHT at Ashford Works on Tuesday 20 September 1966 again. Both the Ashford USAs (the other was MAUNSELL, see next page) were retired from service in 1967 and the following year sold to Woodham's scrapyard at Barry in South Wales. Fortunately, they ran hot and delivery was interrupted at Tonbridge which gave the Kent and East Sussex Railway the opportunity to purchase them. WAINWRIGHT became KESR No 21.

USA class DS237 MAUNSELL at Ashford Works on Tuesday 20 September 1966. It was built at Vulcan Ironworks (USA) in 1943 for the United States Corps of Engineers, with the works number 4441. After the war it spent most of its working life as BR 30065 shunting in Southampton Docks until it was withdrawn in October 1962 and transferred to departmental stock in November 1963.

MAUNSELL again at Ashford Works on Tuesday 20 September 1966. After the war it spent most of its working life as BR 30065 shunting in Southampton Docks until it was withdrawn in October 1962 and transferred to departmental stock in November 1963. The overhead catenaries which can be seen beyond the locomotive pre-dated the HS1 electrification by more than forty years. When the main line was electrified with the third rail system in 1961 they were installed over the sidings (for locomotives) to avoid the danger of accidental contact with the live rail. MAUNSELL became No 22 on the KESR and its first large locomotive in service in 1974.

Bournemouth's Class 3 2-6-2T 82028 heads Maunsell coach set 609, made up of Brake Composite 6694 and Open Second 1353, on the 9:50 Wareham to Swanage branch train past Worgret Junction signal box on Wednesday 8 April 1964. The locomotive was pulling away after slowing down to collect the token for the section to Corfe Castle. Note the goods vans at the rear.

Standard Class 3 2-6-2T 82028 crosses over from the Swanage branch to the main line at Worgret Junction on the 12:30 Swanage to Wareham train on Wednesday 8 April 1964. One of about 14 of the class of 45 allocated at sometime to the Southern Region, it was built at Swindon Works in 1954 and withdrawn in September 1966. Unlike the M7s used on the branch, the Class 3 locomotives had to run round the carriages as they were not auto-fitted.

Redhill 2-6-4T 80094 crosses the Barkham Road level crossing at Wokingham on Friday 1 January 1965. New Year's Day was not a public holiday in England at the time. The train was due to depart from Wokingham at 11:37 and arrive at Reading (Southern) at 11:48. It had left Redhill at 10:18. 80094 was built at Brighton Works in 1954 and was withdrawn in July 1966. Something like a third of the this 155 strong class was allocated to the Southern Region at various times.

7: Ex LSWR Tank Engines

Ex London and South Western Railway William Adams designed 0415 class 4-4-2 radial tank 30584 looks very sorry for itself withdrawn at Eastleigh on Tuesday 28 August 1962. It was built as LSWR 520 by Dübs & Co in 1885 with the works number 2109 and had been withdrawn in January 1961 along with the two other survivors of the class of 71. They had been retained many years after the others to operate the steeply graded, weight restricted and sharply curved Lyme Regis branch.

Ex LSWR 0415 class 30583 was more fortunate than 30584 as it was the only one of its class to be preserved and was chosen out of the three survivors because it still had the original pattern of boiler. It is seen on the Bluebell Railway at Sheffield Park in LSWR livery and with its original number, 488, on a very wet Saturday 20 April 1963. Built by Neilson, Reid & Co in 1885 with the works number 2309, it had been withdrawn by BR in July 1961 and purchased by the Bluebell Railway when Ivatt 2-6-2 tanks took over duties on the Lyme Regis branch.

488 works a one coach train near Horsted Keynes in the early afternoon on Sunday 26 November 1967. 488 was acquired by the Ministry of Munitions in 1917 and used at Ridham Dock in Kent. After the First World War it was sold to Colonel Holman F Stephens for use on the East Kent Railway where it was renumbered 5. When the Southern Railway needed an additional radial tank for the Lyme Regis branch 488 was no longer being used on the EKR so, in March 1946, it was purchased by the SR and overhauled at Eastleigh Works for that branch.

Ex LSWR William Adams designed O2 class 0-4-4T 30199 was built at Nine Elms Works in 1891. It was withdrawn in December 1962 but not cut up until the following December. It is seen here, withdrawn, at Eastleigh on Tuesday 23 April 1963. A number of members of the class remained in service on the Isle of Wight until the end of 1966 but, along with 30225 also withdrawn in December 1962, 30199 was one of the last pair to be in use on the mainland.

DS682 was an Adams G6 0-6-0T built at Nine Elms in 1898. It was numbered 30238 by BR but became departmental stock DS682 when withdrawn from regular service in November 1960 and sent to Meldon ballast quarry in Devon as a shunter. Its work there ended in December 1962 and it was photographed at Eastleigh on Tuesday 23 April 1963 just one month before it was cut up, the last of its class.

Dugald Drummond designed LSWR M7 class 0-4-4T 30667 has arrived at Ash station ready to head the Railway Enthusiasts' Club "Hampshire Hog" railtour on a very wet Saturday 14 March 1964. The tour ran via Aldershot, Bordon, Alton, Winchester City, Eastleigh, Winchester Chesil, Newbury, Didcot, Reading General, Ascot, Chertsey and Woking to Farnborough Main but got off to a bad start because 30667 failed at Ash and was replaced by Q1 class 33035. I was on this trip which turned out to be a long, wet but memorable day.

30667 was relegated to the bay platform at Ash on Saturday 14 March 1964. It seems possible that it was, in fact, 30106 and it had swapped numbers when that locomotive was withdrawn in 1961. The locomotive in the photograph was withdrawn in May 1964 and scrapped at Britton Ferry in Wales. The Southern Premier Division football match at Guildford City's Joseph Road Ground against Bexley United shown on the poster had taken place on 29 February and had been won by the home team: 4-1.

The month before it was withdrawn from service, M7 class 0-4-4T 30053 nears the main line at Worgret Junction on the Swanage branch train on Wednesday 8 April 1964. It had left Swanage at 09:30 and was due to arrive at Wareham at 09:52. 30053 was fitted for push-pull operation so it was ideal for branch line work. It was built Nine Elms Works in 1905 and withdrawn by British Railways in May 1964. In 1967 it was sent to Steamtown, first in Vermont and later at Scranton, Pennsylvania, USA, for preservation. 30053 returned to England in 1987 and was restored to working condition. In 1992 it was reunited with the Swanage Railway.

30053 propels its two coach Maunsell push-pull set 606 (Brake Composite 6678 and Open Second 1328) on its return to Swanage near Worgret Junction on the 11:10 from Wareham on Wednesday 8 April 1964. The end of push-pull workings was near as the branch was soon to be operated by Standard class 3 and 4 and Ivatt 2MT tank engines until dieselisation in 1967. Things were already changing as BR class 3 2-6-2T 82028 was the other locomotive on the branch that day.

30053 pushes its Maunsell set 606 along the main line just before Worgret Junction on Wednesday 8 April 1964. This time it was the 12:26 from Wareham, arriving at Swanage at 12:51. 30053 had only very recently been allocated to Bournemouth shed (71B) and so made available for the Swanage branch. This was only for a short time as it was withdrawn from service, along with the rest of Bournemouth's M7 allocation, at the end of the following month.

30053 has just left the main line to take the Swanage branch at Worgret Junction on the 12:26 from Wareham on Wednesday 8 April 1964. Trains had to slow down when passing the signal box to collect a token for the section to Corfe from the signalman. The Swanage Branch was closed in January 1972 but it has since been reopened and is now operated as a heritage line. Almost incredibly, half a century later the now preserved 30053 is based back home there.

Bournemouth (71B) allocated M7 30480 arrives at Lymington Pier station on Thursday 9 April 1964. The train was being propelled by the push-pull fitted locomotive. Built at Eastleigh, 30480 entered service in 1911 and it was withdrawn the month after this photograph was taken.

30480 stands at Lymington Pier station on Thursday 9 April 1964. It was waiting to depart at 11:18 for the five and a half mile run along the branch to Brockenhurst where it was due to arrive at 11:30. The branch was opened from Brockenhurst to Lymington in 1858 and extended to the Pier station in 1884. It still conveys passengers from the main line connection to the pier where it meets the ferries to Yarmouth on the Isle of Wight.

30480 pulls away from Lymington Pier station on the 11:18 to Brockenhurst on Thursday 9 April 1964. This photograph was taken from the 11:15 ferry which had just started out on its thirty-five minute crossing to Yarmouth on the Isle of Wight. M7s were soon to be replaced by Ivatt Class 2 2-6-2T locomotives for the final few years of steam operation.

Ex LSWR H16 class 4-6-2T 30519 is minus its coupling rods in Feltham shed yard (70B) on Sunday 7 July 1963. Built at Eastleigh Works as one of a small class of five specifically designed by Robert Urie to work trains from the marshalling yards at Feltham, it entered service in 1922. It had already been withdrawn, along with the other four, in November 1962 and it was scrapped three months after this photograph was taken.

Southern Railway Richard Maunsell designed W class 3-cylinder 2-6-4T 31911 was built at Eastleigh Works and it entered service in 1932. It was the first of a class of fifteen designed for freight transfer between yards around London. It had already been withdrawn, in October 1963, when seen here in very poor weather at Eastleigh on Sunday 15 March 1964. It was cut up during the following month.

Ex LSWR William Adams designed B4 class 0-4-0T 30089 stands between two withdrawn M7 locomotives at Eastleigh on Tuesday 23 April 1963. Built as LSWR 89 at Nine Elms Works in 1892 and named TROUVILLE, it had been the shed pilot at Guildford (70C) before being withdrawn in March 1963 and it was scrapped in May 1964. Note that it still carried the "lion on a cycle" BR emblem used from 1948 to 1956.

B4 class 30096 is still in BR service at Eastleigh shed (71A) on Tuesday 23 April 1963. This Adams designed small 0-4-0T was built at Nine Elms in 1893 and named NORMANDY. It had spent its early life as a Southampton Dock shunter until displaced in 1947. Its final BR work was on shunting duty at Winchester goods yard. It was withdrawn in October 1963 and sold to Corralls coal merchants in Southampton.

A year later, on Thursday 9 April 1964, 30096 is working again in Southampton Docks. Seen here at Dibles Wharf, and still looking very much like a BR locomotive, it was now working for Corralls and used to move coal between Northam Yard and Dibles Wharf. It was later painted green and named CORRALL QUEEN. In 1972 it was sold for preservation and it is now to be found on the Bluebell Railway where it was first steamed in 1986.

8: Over the Water to the Isle of Wight

Ex London and South Western Railway O2 class 0-4-4T W26 WHITWELL runs light along the Ryde railway pier on Monday 22 April 1963. It was built at Nine Elms Works as LSWR 210 in 1891 and it was withdrawn in May 1966. Pier Head station can be seen behind the bunker. At this time there was still the opportunity to cross from there to Portsmouth on one of the ex Southern Railway paddle steamers RYDE or SANDOWN or one of the post war ferries MV SHANKLIN, SOUTHSEA or BRADING. Southsea is just visible in the distance across the Solent.

O2 class W33 BEMBRIDGE trundles along the Ryde railway pier bound for Cowes respecting, presumably, the 20mph speed restriction on Monday 22 April 1963. It was built at Nine Elms Works as LSWR 218 in 1892 and it was withdrawn in December 1966. The photograph was taken from Ryde Pier which was originally opened in 1814, long before the parallel 1880 railway pier which still carries trains. The rails that can be seen between these two piers are on the now closed tramway pier. The Victorian pavilion with its dome was demolished in 1971 and the Pier Head signal box was taken out of use in 1974.

O2 class W32 BONCHURCH and W16 VENTNOR are in steam on Ryde shed (70H) on Monday 22 April 1963. Both these 0-4-4 tank locomotives were built at Nine Elms Works in 1892. W32 was originally LSWR 226 and it was withdrawn in October 1964. W16, LSWR 217, was withdrawn in December 1966. Ryde shed was next to St John's Road station and the site has now become the station car park.

O2 class W21 SANDOWN arrives at the end of its journey at Ryde St John's Road station at 17:27 on the 17:08 from Newport on Thursday 9 April 1964. Built at Nine Elms Works as LSWR 205 in 1891, SANDOWN was withdrawn in May 1966.

O2 class W36 CARISBROOKE was built at Nine Elms Works in 1891 as LSWR 198. It became W36 on the Isle of Wight in 1949 and it was withdrawn in June 1964. It stood in Ryde St John's Road station on a Ventnor train on Monday 22 April 1963. Ventnor trains were indicated by the single disc above the smokebox door. Ryde Works can be seen on the right. It has now become the depot for Island Line electric trains and the brick part is a listed grade 2 building.

O2 class W27 MERSTONE at Ryde St John's Road station waiting to depart on the 17:35 to Cowes, where it was due to arrive at 16:09, on Thursday 9 April 1964. This train only started from Pier Head in the Summer service. Cowes trains were indicated by the two discs above the buffers. W27 was built at Nine Elms Works as LSWR 184 in 1890. The Westinghouse brake fitted to the O2s working on the Isle of Wight can be seen on the right-hand side of the smokebox.

W27 MERSTONE nears Ryde St John's Road, where it was due to arrive at 16:58, on the 16:21 Cowes departure on Thursday 9 April 1964. This train continued to Pier Head only in the Summer service. MERSTONE was withdrawn after it had been at the rear of the last BR steam train on the island, on 31 December 1966. The O2s on the Isle of Wight had larger bunkers than those on the mainland.

O2 class W29 ALVERSTONE has just left Ryde St John's Road on the Isle of Wight on the 16:29 Ryde Esplanade to Ventnor, where it was due to arrive at 17:14, on Thursday 9 April 1964. It was built at Nine Elms Works as LSWR 202 in 1891 and withdrawn in May 1966. Ex LBSCR Brake coach S4156 was part of set No 492.

O2 class W18 NINGWOOD heads the 16:08 Ryde St John's Road to Ventnor just a short distance along the line towards Smallbrook Junction on Thursday 9 April 1964. W18 was built at Nine Elms Works as LSWR 220 in 1892 and withdrawn in December 1965. Despite appearances, this was not a traditional section of double track. It was, in effect, operated as two parallel single lines and Ventnor trains used the left hand line to Smallbrook Junction where the two branches separated.

O2 class W35 FRESHWATER has just left Ryde St John's Road on the 16:35 to Cowes, where it was due to arrive at 15:09, on Thursday 9 April 1964. W35 was built at Nine Elms Works as LSWR 181 in 1890 and withdrawn in October 1966. This train started from Pier Head during the Summer timetable only. Cowes trains used the right hand line to Smallbrook Junction.

O2 class W14 FISHBOURNE looks very smart apparently ex works in the siding at Sandown, with W18 NINGWOOD and W17 SEAVIEW behind, on Monday 22 April 1963. It was built at Nine Elms Works as LSWR 178 in 1889 and withdrawn after it had carried a wreath on the final BR steam train to run on the Isle of Wight. This was the 21:40 (which was 14 minutes late) from Shanklin to Ryde on 31 December 1966 with W27 at the rear.

O2 class W30 SHORWELL pulls into Sandown station on a Ventnor train on Monday 22 April 1963 while my mother waits patiently on a bench with my tartan duffle bag. It was built at Nine Elms Works as LSWR 219 in 1892 and withdrawn in September 1965. The line from Ryde to Sandown was opened to passengers by the Isle of Wight Railway on 23 August 1864 and is still served by Island Line electric trains to Shanklin. The final section to Ventnor was closed in 1966.

W35 FRESHWATER arrives at Newport station on the 13:21 Cowes to Ryde Pier Head, where it was due to arrive at 14:05, on Thursday 9 April 1964. Newport station was opened by the Cowes and Newport Railway in 1862 and was closed to passengers in February 1966 when services from Ryde to Cowes ceased. It was demolished to make way for the Newport by-pass. Note the extensive yards and carriage sidings.